LITTLE BLACK TRAIN

Poems

JORDAN SMITH

THREE MILE HARBOR PRESS

NEW YORK

Three Mile Harbor Press
PO Box 1
Stuyvesant, New York 12173
www.3mileharborpress.com

ISBN: 978-0-9983406-4-7

Library of Congress Control Number: 2020932689

First Edition
Printed in the United States of America

Cover art: "Political Needs" by Walter Hatke, 2019
Cover design by Pamela Hughes
© All Rights Reserved

For Malie, always

CONTENTS

ONE

TWO

THREE

ONE

Sign Shift

— Astrology is something else. It is not science (NASA)

Above the fence, the trees, winter's sky, the stars
Are changing, the stories have shifted a little, some of us
Are not what we thought, some of us are short of breath
From this cold, some virgins are lions now, some scales
Balance only innocence and find it wanting. Some of us
Have lost a twin. Some measure each breath, grave as Socrates
Weighing the hemlock in his hand. He knew when choice is
gone,
What's left is what's given, and who can trust that?

Fuck

— *In Ireland, "fuck" is like a comma."* (Adrian Frazier)

I say it more now, usually when I'm watching the news.
A poem almost, that lyric *condensare*,
Of the whole of speech, not a part, not a verb
For what in a novel might occur at most a few times
In a later chapter, after a long wait, a small
And private part of life, if much anticipated.

And not a noun either, as in Miller, Mailer,
Subject and object conflated, pronounced
After a celebratory inhalation,
Like satisfaction after a long, surly deprivation,
And so preening, ungrateful, the vowel clipped
Short of surprise or pleasure: mere consonance.

Now, right now, the announcer finishing her story
Of horror, stupidity, it is an explosion
Through the teeth, unwilled, a little death
Of meaning, a little death of hope, hardly
Dulled by repetition, indifference, well-meaning,
All I've got, quick and dirty, said and done.

My Politics Fall Apart Again

— Perduta... Perdona

In Act 3 of *Figaro*, when Mozart gives all the grandeur of the
aristocracy to the servants in his marriage march,

Fine flourishes, and nothing in it of parody, of clowns trampling
down the meter at the feast, of the sham

Ceremony the Count intends, of Cherubino's campy disguise,
like Achilles curtseying among the women...

No, it is all sorted now,

As if there were another world in this one, or would be except
for this sudden sadness.

I have lost it, Barbarina sings, and that is the unease in the
gavotte, a plot to follow, elegant, courtly,

Forgiving only when forgiveness is what keeps the old order in
place, and how easily we acquiesce to what we always knew,

We for whom loss is only a syllable or two removed from
pardon.

The History Plays

Are brutality configured for a plot's trajectory, deformity as
character (that is, as tragedy), and the crown as the torture-
master's tightening band,

Elegance as a fall's prefiguration, kindness as strategic error,
mercy... Well, mercy doesn't enter into it, not where time is a
wave, cresting, breaking,

And all you love or might have loved caught, not where the
undertow has carried all the armored bodies down
the coast where the fleet is gathering,

But here, in the loss of detail in your sons' faces that is twilight
on the marshes, in their hands on the sword hilts,

Which are traces of salt in the spray. And treason? Treason is
the salt's wound, Treason is the gull's cry, greedy, repetitive,
self-justifying.

See, you have already ordered the crossing, the disembarkation.

See, the wind is fair, that would cover your footsteps.

A Gift of Afghan Tea

— for Jamal Aram

I make it strong tonight, with cardamom, a little honey.
I want to be awake when the news breaks,
Whatever it is.

The friend who gave me this tea lives in exile in Toronto,
Waiting, writing another story.
His pen's flourish, a diacritical mark
Above the name of an unremarkable hamlet,
Modifies the hyperbole of empire.

I've been reading the books on grand strategy,
Shrugging, resigned commentaries on the great game.
A fine debacle leading to a minor if foreseen lament.

The little scrim of oil trembles on the surface
Of glass of tea on a table,
A tinny transistor radio tuned to anything at all
Since anything might happen.

On the Suicides at the NY/Canada Border

Yes, they step in the same river twice.
They present their bad passports, their reasons, their distracted
evasions.
 No, they will not be staying long, they tell the customs agents.
There are a thousand islands where they might reconsider,
Some with ruined castles, some with cabins that would have
cramped Thoreau.
They stumble at the questions about age and destination. They
swear allegiance
Too easily to our anger and our pity; they profess to honor
The deserters from the unjust war. They've had enough of
fighting.
They imagine a city of bistros, accordions, tables on the
sidewalks,
But it is under snow. They are safe. No tourist will mistake them
for a compatriot.
In the bar, the old violinist plays a song that's not sad enough,
And they share his panic as the notes fall off pitch. His fingers
are stiff.
They share his suffering. They forgive his dissonance.
They forgive the fog, the geese that pass so loudly overhead.
They are in a position to forgive all imperfection, all transience,
to forgive even us,
Burdened with our snapshots and souvenirs, who will not join
them,
Not yet, at the café of good intentions and unmeant
consequences
Where they have fallen—is it sleep?—into and in spite of our
sorrow.

A Cancelled Flight to Granada

— for Bern Kuhn

I don't know which moved me most of what I did not see,
The sublimity of the vista over the old city
Or the desolate, melancholic intimacy of the poet's studio.

On the one hand, the light was golden, was russet, was sunset
(In the stock footage, at least), and on the other
The auburn and cream tile floor, the auburn and ivory piano,
The chair with the elegantly curved arms

And that same light through the windows.
What city is not what Freud said Rome is, a sort of hologram
Of past above past below past, and what room is not, and what
hands
That lift from the keyboard in disappointment, in rancor,

Shaking, and the failure of the divine to appear is so much dust
To be brushed away, so many days,
So many empires.

Then, after coffee, the flight cancelled,
One day drawn
From the deck of unwritten postcards, and then another.

Interior, With Window, With Wind

— for Mikhail Lossel

A scarred wooden table, a blue and gray enamel cup, a Shaker
chair.
A notebook, or
At least the sentiment of one. A pen, uncapped.

Shutters, unshuttered. A horizon line of trees or dunes.
You see, sentiment. And solitude, a closure, a cloister,
Although, somewhere, a door swings open.

The wind would explain that
If it had any explanation at all to offer.

Lorca's Mercedes

Black, of course.
Even the numerals on the license, the charcoal-numbered
gauges.

He has purloined it from the mayor, that unregenerate
Falangist,
The one who decreed the end of measure.

How modern, the words on the proclamations.
They are a taste in his mouth, rubber streaked on asphalt.

The cheap black tobacco one worker offers another
Is his small blessing.

What hero publishes the account of his descent, grudging,
What sort of man attends a funeral to count the flowers in the
wreaths?

He cannot tell the olive grove from the alley's black end.
It is all one to him.

The precision of the pistons in their dark oil,
Deep in the cavern of the engine, there are steps he must
count.

America, a Trance

Don't think this is over.
The fiddler's got another hundred trips through
Goin' to That Free State left in his bow arm

And another dozen anecdotes about how it doesn't mean
What you think it does.
It sounds like it's about freedom. It's about memory,
And those unforgiveable injuries, taxes and rents.

Thoreau's master surveyor whacked the boy with a switch
So he'd never forget the boundary corner.
He got paid enough to do that.

The fiddler has one squint eye
And the kind of seriousness you don't find much anymore
Until you do, and it's too late;
He's into a set of cross-A tunes that might end Sunday
If it ends at all.

See, you're learning it his way:
Sitting by the wood stove, sweating, bow a little slack,
Gut strings, and nothing written down.
If there's a dog at your feet, a glass by your hand,

You earned it, playing the same damn tune.

Little Black Train

I never made it to San Francisco, '55 or '67, to Soho
Or the East Village, to Brooklyn with Whitman or Miller or
Auden.
Instead I'm driving through Waterford, New York, toward North
Troy,
Listening to an artist pitch his memoir of good times in the
Seventies

On the radio, and because he can't put two clear sentences
together,
And because the rest of the news is murder on the one hand
And on the other
I switch to an old Appalachian song, a brutal,
Christian exhortation to *fix your business right*.

What I miss in these little towns are the grade crossings
Where you had to stop when the gates dropped
And the squat bulk of one of the black New York Central diesels
pulled through,
Then the freights, with their old-fashioned graffiti,
A tramp's scrawled skull and bones or a half-gone *Jesus...*

What I miss is the weight of it, just a few feet from the car's
grille,
The shock of wind and metal, whatever couldn't be stopped,
not for anything,
When I wasn't going anywhere at all.

Upstate, the Thirties

— remembering stories from Carl Carmer's *Listen
for a Lonesome Drum*

He's slung the boots he used to polish for church, the laces tied
together, around his neck while he fords the stream,

Guitar case held high. He's got no place to sleep and the houses
he remembers are open to the sky, wardrobes and brass bed
frames streaked with the rain.

He takes the turn up the road above Vine Valley following the
wheel tracks until the lake is out of sight, and then in the gully
below the vineyard,

A meeting, and all the Italian pickers with their bottles of
grappa are talking, the words translated so a few German
mechanics and roofers,

And the old IWW guys still talking direct action, can listen in.
Maybe they'll even sing a little before that well-dressed rep
from the one union or another gets going, sounding,

He thinks, about as right and wrong as any true believer at any
revival tent. He has played those too, and the best time was
once after the testifying, the laying on of hands,

With some whiskey and a couple of rounds of some tune
everyone knows the chords to, and a girl who remembered the
words to "Red Wing"

Whispered into his ear *solidarity forever* before they walked off
behind the tents.

America Just Ends

In this photograph of a lumberyard, a gas station, a hardware
store with a railroad siding around back.

Beyond, the land rises, and you're in a Robert Frost poem one
of the grim ones, or *The Hills Have Eyes*,

Everyone passing through is a tourist, and the local word for
traveler translates as either *mark* or *marked.*

So stick to the road, as far as your gas or credit will take you.
Either way, just before one thing or another runs out,

And you hear the chorus starting up "Shall We Gather at the
River" in the sunset in your rearview mirror,

You'll wish you were back at the counter, setting down the
brown paper bag of washers and bolts,

Telling that girl in your flatlander's accent that you have a few
more things to find in the narrow aisles,

So put these on the tab, and she makes a note and tucks it in
the tube of that track and cable affair they haven't made since
the forties,

And it shoots back to the cashier who stamps it payment due
and stuffs it in the same little file

They've kept since the first time you walked in the place and
said there were some things you needed to fix up,

If you could just remember where you put the goddamned list,
and she laughed, because it was right there in your hand.

The Comforting Weight of Monopoly

In your hand, the thimble, the shoe, the flatiron, the terrier (so like FDR's Fala), the racing car, the top hat, Depression domesticity, with a leaven of the old 1920s lush brashness,

And then the dice, yellowed as ivory passed from hand to hand, heavy until you let them rattle onto the table or the still mostly empty board, into the moment when chance sets its course (if chance can set a course), plunging

Like a bad day on the market or at the track, into the insubstantial, promissory premises, money as flimsy as tissue, denominations uncorrected for inflation, and the thumbed, softening cardboard of the deeds, flipped again and again,

And then of course the other players take their turns; you see it as they hold the dice a little longer than they need to, as they heft their pieces before counting out their moves. It is Eden, that moment; there is no separation between them and all they want,

Since that is all there is. And then it is yours, it might be, it ever shall be, at least until you recall how much scrambling it takes once you've set out on that path that always returns

To the small usual reward, so you pick up the dice, you might as well, and take their weight one more time in your hands.

Grandeur

The books I used to read,
R.D. Laing and N.O. Brown and Graves and Jung, most of all,
Jung
Which gave my ordinary, late adolescent unhappiness a touch
of grandeur,
Sell for pennies on the internet now.
And of whom should I ask forgiveness
For the misuses I put them to?

The roughshod pursuit of words was one,
And the hero's arrogance,
Which was whim or grievance or desire,
Each misunderstood
According to whim or grievance or desire.

The shadows of the trees should have been enough,
Or the woman in that Ritsos poem,
Slicing thin circles of lemon.

No wonder I wrote little and worked hard at it,
Without a word of praise from my difficult masters
Who had retreated into such solitude
As I wished for myself
In their company.

The Teacher

Orpheus in reverse, he stands behind her while she reads.
He counts her syllables.

But for his politeness
He would have preceded her down those forbidding stairs,

Yet in the depths of their marble, sea-dark and sea-scoured,
Where would he find his footing

If not by following her measure, a falling rhythm
Caught in the iambs' syncopations?

When she found her gift, that almost casual backward glance,
What was left for him to teach her?

Only the geography of their island. Well, he had thought it theirs.
Such arrogance. Even now,

He does not quite see it, not even in the mirror
He took her for.

Pays du Haut

You sang of violence, and it was nothing, was easy.
Since you lived in that high country. And love,

Your hopeless, insistent love of the unobtainable...
You knew a pretext when you saw it, knew

When all her loveliness was a field of yarrow and wild mustard
Where she loosed the dogs, and you danced, wolf,

Towards the cliff's edge. Sing of that, troubadour,
Sing of it as if it had been your hands, not hers,

That placed the flayed skin on your shoulders.
Let hers stay simply clasped on the embroidered hem of her
cloak,

For who would blame such beauty?
Sing sweetly that we may understand.

Poetica

Bennington, morning, July, breakfast in the inn with J and L
L suggests a walk, across the green...
Well, *sward* is the word that comes to mind, somehow,
And produces (from where?) a parasol,
Raising it just when we're in clear sight of the terrace and the center
Of the sun-struck frame, moving through art's
History of proportion and perspective, although her prop
And the splotchy, summery green hills and the flowerbeds
And our air of intently experienced leisure gesture toward the Impressionists.
We are poets, that couldn't be clearer, and now we are in a poem
That you are reading as you are finishing your omelet, your coffee,
And happen to look across the field, curious or annoyed.
Our artifice will leave it to you to wonder what the plot is,
The rising action, the conversation, the circumstances, when really
It is only the composition that matters, a trio in summer light,
Just exactly enough.

A Suite of Ghosts

The first read the palm
Of the handsomest, least scrupulous man at the party.
He took his time
With the ambiguities.

The second petted the Siamese cat in his lap,
Heavily, drawing out her purrs.
His hands bronzed and thick from work
On the unfinished house, the undone manuscript.
He expounded on *The Republic*
With the air of a tourist
After a brief, unsatisfactory visit.

The third had long, silver hair, as beautiful as his ex-wife's
(and she was famous for it).
If all is vanity, whose is greater, he asked the mirror,
And so his self-regard foundered,
In the pejoratives of close comparison.

When the fourth shaved his head,
It was as a parable for his initiates
That their contrition might be compared
To the voluptuous restraint of their master,
His solitude guarded
By disciples shed one by one.

All gone now, gone or merely out of style,
And their words,
The by-blows of their ecstasies...
Recalled now with that vagueness
Nostalgia only accentuates.

Who Would Have Thought the Saxophone

— for Charles Lloyd

In the high school band room, the sax section runs over their
parts, no breath, just fingers on the fine-tooled keys,

Clump and clack of pads and brass, pure early modern
mechanics, Adam Smith's pin- makers laboring

In service of a great music of commerce, each silent and intent,
as a century passes like nothing, like a fife tune,

And somewhere a march is stirring, somewhere someone
imagines a reedy, gut-born tone,

Undercutting the splendid assurance of the cornet, honking at
the euphonium's platitudes, and as always,

Although the argument is efficiency and the underwriters
(Fokker, Enfield) smart in parade dress,

There is more at stake: the airman's barrel roll for the pleasure
of the civilians on the ground before the strafing, the
infantryman's poems jammed in his haversack,

Then Bechet's soprano, then the massed sax sections of swing,
the cutting sessions, the aspirants and acolytes

Trying out their fingerings at a side table at the club, Chicago, a
couple of white guys in plaid and khaki cheering from the
sidelines;

In a cottage on Milvia Street in Berkeley, the click and clatter of
typewriter keys,

And at Big Sur, an old man with a horn under his arm has walked a little further into the scrub where the trail dodges back from the cliff

Considering that long paradox of infinite division. Who would have thought the broken might contrive such beauty.

Who would have thought the saxophone might be one voice of god.

TWO

Eight Hats

— after the paintings of Walter Hatke

1. Soldier

"That's all that's left of Modernism, the way it takes it all apart
and lets you see how broken we are, how little protects us,

And how cheaply. A few leather straps and a cowl, some
netting, all sweat stained and ready to split or tear or chafe, and
then the helmet. Drab and flat, and what good would it do you?

Any marksman would aim below its rim, and shrapnel spreads.
You know men were killed just by the concussion from the
shells?

Irony doesn't stand up much better than steel to that kind of
knowledge.

How long do you think we'll put up with it? Pretty much forever,
I'd say, as long as the market can turn even *Guernica* to
collateral

For the debt we've racked up to make a few people comfortable
and the rest suitable subjects."

— World War 1 helmet

35

2. Crusher

"My father-in-law wore one on his farm, near Booneville, near Port Leyden, near the Black River falls.

Half a brain between them, he said when we drove past the two brothers who ran the sawmill arguing by the road, the bigger one

Tossing the keys to the truck in the dirt, pushing the hunter's hat he grabbed from the gun rack in the back further up on his head,

Sticking out his thumb, waiting for someone northbound to pick him up,

Not all that far from where just a few months back the two convicts went on the run, breaking into cabins, finding dope and home-made whiskey, a shotgun.

With that much cunning, you'd think they'd end up in Montreal or Burlington or some other idea of paradise, but you know the story

Never ends like that, between the black flies and the bogs, the booze and a country that doesn't reward much beyond a stubborn settling in,

And, as the old apology for a misfired joke goes, *you'd have to be there to get it.* And if you were, you'd still be, drinking raw spirits out of someone else's smudged jelly glass, smoking that cheap stuff from his backlot patch, checking the ammo and the local news,

Wondering why, if they were so damned intent on catching you, they were looking everywhere else but here,

The first place they should have expected and the last."

— *Plaid hunting cap*

3. Academe

"He always said the key was to just show up. Most people were too polite to chuck you straight out the door, and the good liberals who ran those places would never play the class card,

Not in any obvious way. He knew how to use that. He smoked everywhere and said with great pleasure the worst things to the wrong people, a test,

You either got it or you didn't, and behind his tweed and irony and flash, was scrap and ripped denim from years he didn't want to talk about, not until those last poems.

What he wanted in return was candor, perfect, the kind Whitman said was the always unpunched ticket to forgiveness.

Give him that and he'd look at you as if there was nothing else to know between you, so why not have a drink, the good stuff,

But after a few, whatever he said just touched the conversation at a tangent, touched, then dropped

Towards some chasm where no one could join him, and any reply was the marginalia in a poorly translated copy of the *Inferno*,

A circle around whose boundlessness those who had confessed and those who would not wound like metaphors around a subject whose difficulty was exactly that."

— *Academic tam*

4. Summer: Miami

— I will die in Miami in the sun... (Donald Justice)

"A white straw hat with a black crown band should tell you
something about the connection between glare and mourning.

If funerals are often overcast, that is a matter of courtesy. Who
would wish to look too closely at the hands gripping the flowers,
cupping the marl, the rails of the casket,

Since grasping is never attractive. And who does not dress well
for the occasion?

Only the odd cousin, in his stained khaki suit, his cheap clip-ons
and garish tie with the slovenly knot

Of someone who has forgotten that elegance is also a kind of
propriety, or perhaps never knew. Or perhaps his contempt (for
what, and what have we done that it should fall on us?) is so
great

That when, at the reading of the will, he finds he has been
named executor, he rubs his glasses on his tie, fingers the key to
the safe deposit, signs the papers and pockets them, like a
broker accepting a finder's fee,

And walks out, where it is sunny now, and the sweat gathers at
the rim of his broken-crowned Panama, and he sits on a folded
newspaper on a bench in one of those parks

Until his bus comes. And that is the last we hear of him, despite
all the lawyers and the probate judge and the accountants
who only tell us what we knew: the trust is empty, the reward
of surviving is that costs accumulate, the only legacy

Is the hat he left on the bench, battered and sweaty and out of style, but something to keep you from the sun."

— Panama

5. Trekker

"Now that it's mostly where I might have gone, I like the edges
of the old topo maps the best: widening, descending contour
lines, and then the perpendicular, blank corner's

Horizon, where whatever is beyond, is out of sight, out of mind,
as it should be, the teachers say in their obscure poems of the
particular, since there's plenty

Of detail to be concerned about in the moment's quadrant: that
farm road, just a hatched line, that rounds the face of the bluff
where the marked trail heads catastrophically up toward a
ledge

That might be an orchid's lair, rare, or the cave's lip for Dante's
great cat that drives the trekker in his pilgrim's oilcloth hat, the
key to his worldly store tucked in the sweatband,

Down, since that seems the easier way until you see how the
pattern you've watched from so high above swirls and blends in
that cleft of infinite regression, and upwards, after so much
struggle, the higher ground simply vanishes,

And somewhere below the clouds you're above now is the
middle path, well-worn and mostly lost, since commerce has
gone elsewhere, and the apple trees nestle between
oak and scrub,

And with a little patience you might sit there and let it all come
to you."

— *Oilcloth cruiser*

41

6. Political Needs

— Et in Arcadia ego

"I prefer nostalgia—*I too was in Acadia*—to the darkness behind it, but that's sentiment over history, holiday bunting draping the war memorial as the fire department band breaks ranks and heads for the beer truck,

And if anyone notices that the statue is listing a little, the grounds crew will be around after the speeches to shore it up with a couple of cinder blocks, good enough for government work,

And meanwhile the pols on the podium are having it their own way, which is the virtue of rhetoric's vices, that everyone else has to shut up. Look, it's my hometown, I know it, and if I never went back to the Congregational Church

For another flag-bordered sermon that didn't mention the war or the riots downtown, it's not that I've forgotten anything: the parades along the canal side, the morning glories on the 19th century columns, the WPA mural of harvest, of bounty, above the checkout desk of the public library.

That's the key, right there. You make a promise about what the past is like, and that story remains

As much or as little a lie as evening's darkening, a depth of purple prose eclipsing something as determinedly cheerful

As the colors of liberty wrapped around a straw boater's crown, a hat you can't wear except in the fairest of weather."

— Straw boater with red, white, and blue ribbon

7. Prague

"The task of the keepers of memory is arduous, and not only
because the destruction was so great, but because the
fragments are so many.

Who will invoke that scattered congregation?

Who will take as their study the city of the learned, of the
watchful, for whom the expostulations of the word, the
disputations,

Implied, for the attentive, that gesture by which those first
exiles were summoned to embroider, with labor, with patience
and endless uncertainty,

The creation which paradise had otherwise left imperfect?"

— Embroidered yarmulke

8. Yardman

— Bach, Brandenburg #2, for Peter Heinegg

"The thing about the contingent self is that it can be just this beautiful, the recorder, lost up to now behind the trumpet and oboe,

Suddenly breaking clear, a creek between reeds and beds of bell-shaped marsh flowers, all of which must be *meant*, you nod in approval,

A gardener's hand, although listen too closely and you'll hear the numbers working themselves out, which is the problem with design:

Good intentions, and we know how that goes. If I want a self perfect enough for this music, then so much for the failures I find so endearing,

And so much for the attrition that excuses so much so easily, and if I don't, then how will I find

The true path, the one the yardman in his straw hat and grass-stained khakis has made so plain that, like the quiet girl at a dance,

No one would choose it first, just as no one knows how the treble recorder can sing until we tire of flourishes, of sonority,

And turn back to something so brief it must be beautiful, if it is to be at all."

— Shaker straw hat

44

THREE

Early Music

In Paris, from above the Rue des Arquebusiers, I watched
A pro-Morsi demonstration
On the Rue Beaumarchais.
That was before the Bataclan, but only a few blocks away,
The borrowed apartment
So hot in mid-July we kept the windows open
Despite the wasp-swarm of mopeds.

The house had lodged the Count Cagliostro,
Imposter, forger, low-born confidante of the powerful,
Who no more belonged in that comfort than I did,
Who might have enjoyed the plot's twist,
Arrested in the affair of the queen's necklace,
The one fraud he hadn't committed.

So hot, I never took the walk I planned
To the store selling antique musical instruments
Not far from the Hotel de Ville,
Viols and traversi from before the revolution,
A bassoon "unplayed for two centuries,"
The website said,
From a time when the players were servants or worse.

Even a kit fiddle,
The revel master's tool. Not quite a violin,
But plausible, portable
For a peasant turned performer, to lead
His betters in a fine dance,
Effective, as is all irony,
Only when the old order so diminished
That mockery might serve some purpose,
Small instrument though it is and out of date
And useless
In all the clamor that follows.

Traverso

Each note, they say, in praise or frustration has its own color
and timbre,
Is off-pitch to its own degree,

And then there is the player's angle of attack, the nick
Of wind across the embouchure, its undercutting, the humidity
in the room,

The tone wood's density of remembrance, the smoothness or
otherwise
Of the bore, the maker's diagrams of diameter and taper

Drawn from history or experience, the slight inaccuracies of
antique brass calipers
And keys, and all the approximations of design

Allowing cross-fingered accidentals, lipped or not into some
ideal
Temperament, that is, some compromise

Between concentration and diffusion, the center and
circumference
Of breath drawn into a turbulence of air

Man Reading Lacan

Laconic? I can't tell. He's alone
At a table in the functional, touristy, comfortable
La Bohème café in comfortable, touristy Barcelona.
His hair cropped short, his beard long,
Intent as a lover on a book called just *Lacan*.

Why is it so difficult to differentiate intent from boredom?
It would be a relief if he would bend a page,
Or lick a pencil's tip and make a note in the margin,
Or order another café con leche, or pay his tab.
It is as dull as hearing lovers discourse on their love.
Of course, they have nothing for us.

Of course he has nothing for me.
In the doubled mirrors in this café,
The frames go on and on, the subject gets smaller and smaller,
A relief that it need not vanish, not quite
In the street's bustle and dodge, the eccentric traffic,
The exchange rates, visas, and Visas.

Across the Street from the Miro Foundation

In your flowered dress, my love, with that blazing hibiscus
behind you,
You must be at the wrong museum.
You belong downtown, at the *Museu de Modernisme*
With the painting of the regatta, of the mother and daughter at
a window,
With the stained-glass flora, and the dancers in finely inlaid
wood.
In Gaudi's city, there's a lot to be said for the decorative arts,
For the wedding of pleasure and utility.

Not that you or I are decorative, merely, and we're avoiding
usefulness,
At least as I compose the scene with my camera, two seasoned,
Obvious tourists in a landscape, with the composure
Of the bourgeoisie who lived in those paintings, with that
furniture.
There's a lot to be said for accepting elegance
When it comes your way.

Inside, my favorite Miro is a blank, off-white, textured field with
a single tiny...
Well, what would you call it?
Not well defined enough to be a dot; too flat for a sphere, not
as linear as a pulsation
A sort of subatomic emanation of blue, concentrating, or
diffusing.
And then there are the canvases he painted, burned, painted
some more.

Once *modernisme* was the dance of light through a stained-
glass window
On the floor of a room where the problems of comfort
Had been left behind, left to others,

But on the video Miro and his assistant take a torch to it
Until the stretchers show.

You aren't there. You have found a room with Japanese prints,
And on the monitor, a single carver makes cuts as brief, as
precise as breath,
Another and another, until the series of blocks
Is ready for the ink of sky caught in her mirror, in the blue of her
robe
And the red of petals printed there or resting,
A single branch in the vase on her dressing table.

Berggasse 19

A dark passage. Behind the door,
The stairway to the second floor,
But first a glimpse through the arched gate,
High summer's garden. The doctor waits

Inside a room that is all loss
Accounted for, the fine embossed
Volumes, Egyptian deities,
And, most of all, the dignity

You shrug off, as a model must
Her clothes…is it trust or lust
Or both? The only difference
Is shame. And then the transference,

As sweet a betrayal or as crude
As a round dance, or an interlude,
An hour, say, in some hotel
Where each lover tries at last to tell

Some lie that isn't, some truth that is
The last, at last, on that long list.
Come to the end, each thinks, and then
No more hand-wringing, no more amends

Or fear-struck hours or waking dreams,
Each nightmare revealed for what it seems,
Not what it is: an act of pardon,
Before we go back through the garden.

Two Movies, Three Transgressions

— for David St. John

Brideshead. The Dreamers. There is a great house,
An unexpected arrangement; a moment, a manner of meeting.
Brother, sister, friend of my youth. Instructions
For lovers (not yet), a protocol for seeing, for memory,
For the accidental which is also the most practiced. There is a
veil,
But we are allowed this glimpse, and so the first
Transgression is nearly the second: the wish to see
Becomes the sight, becomes only what remains
Of nobility: its willfulness, its audience. Not the dress
Circle dozing through *Pelleas* and the long *diminuendo*,
Not indifference, or all its commonplace misapprehensions,
Nor the familiar, shrugged hope that it will all end badly
enough.
It is sentiment we're left with, as if all those scandals
Were only a means to linger in the presence of something
Like pleasure, something, like salvation we were called
To witness, nodding assent to its poor tangled (gone,
And none too soon) shadows until the lights came on.

One Too Many Samurai Movies

The shakuhachi player in monk's robes with that wicker
Basket over his head as he walks the forest path downward
Toward a stream, never putting a foot wrong on the slick
Granite, and the old man with his tenkara rod and fly
Lifting a trout like a silver sliver from the quick water…
They are nothing, your master would tell you, but appearances.
And if, poor and stubborn student, you argue again
That the apparition of that tiny crevasse still caught
Your heel, kept you from tumbling to the cliff's edge and
learning
More about emptiness than he could teach you, leaving
Your ankle swollen and your, he can't resist adding,
Ignorance intact, well, when the musician drops the basket
To gather the head he has been sent to collect, and the
fisherman
Puts his rod in the streamside bracken and picks up the fine
Blade of which the monk's sword is an echo, you would do well
To look at the moon and think how all beauty is only
Transitory because it has finally occurred to us that we too
Might join our brothers to assault that brigand's castle,
Although his army is many and his ways deceitful, and we
Will go armed like a beggar in the night, the one who craved
A taste, no more, of that rice cake, and with each bite
The moon grew smaller until it was the point of light, just
That, at the very tip of the blade no one knew he had.

Mother of Pearl

— divine intervention, always my intention (Bryan Ferry)

Now whenever Roxy Music comes on the shuffle play
I think of my friend in Baltimore
At the head of the table, our stack of manuscripts
In front of him, his head cocked, his hand poised
Between the elegance of critique and that intent
Disinterested invitation, as if to ask,
What can you show me now?

We all had cigarettes, coffee in stained mugs.
We had leather jackets, beat-up thrift-shop tweeds,
We had good lines, lucky accidents,
Ambitions above our stations,
But elegance, intent?

I could bluff my way through films and jazz and Crane's
visionary company.
I witnessed the persistence of the pearled sunrise above the
Seaman's Mission
And the miraculous appearance of a Johnny-on-the-Spot
In a construction site just this side of Fells Point.

But what I wanted was an unearned grace
Where between word and world the difference was as slight
As a gesture not yet begun, a singer's voice in memory, praising
Artifice, as naturally as that.

Sketches for a Novel

— after paintings from the National Gallery of Ireland

1. The Sun-shade

Her face is perfect for a novel's cover,
The sort I admire, not the sort I read
Straight through or even finish. See how light hovers,
Diffused by the parasol, around her head.
That's what the style would be, a sort of summer
Shimmer of bourgeois sentiment, made dimmer,

Refined by the restraint of its expression.
Her face. Her face is where the trouble starts,
She draws the eye, the light. She thinks repression's
An unasked-for gift of character, a part
She takes; she wants the whole made whole.
The cost's the plot. A letter delayed, the snow

Last April, a bet on the wrong horse.
Enough to start. It hardly matters now.
The style's the thing. The way things take their course,
The hue and cry, are nothing to the slow
Press of her hands along the sunshade's shaft,
As if possession were both curse and craft.

2. The Fair

The fair is faces, horseflesh, cider, wagers,
Tweed and twill, tinkers, a press, good odds
Or long, the start, the swells, a surfeit, pages
From the turf accountants' ledgers, nods
And winks, a band for reels, and over there
An old song lifting: *She moves through the fair.*

She does. She wears a sweater against the chill,
A hat against scrutiny. The man who bumps her arm,
Rushing to place his bet, stops, stands stock still.
There's history between them; there's harm
Unwished for, done like a deal, dun-colored skies
Walked under, endured, *after a pleasant guise*

Quoted, out of context, teas or balls
Or hunts. He's a false start. He is the rumor
Of a good horse running last. Her escort calls
Her back. She shies and turns, a reel, *The Humors
Of the Fair*, she whistles it. He answers,
And they're off, out of the gate. Her gait? A canter.

3. Sunlight

No tragedy without burlesquerie,
She thinks in the hotel bed. Rare. The sun,
That is, this time of year in this wet country.
Her skin too, her flank, rare as steak. A pun
She allows herself, just one indulgence
A woman may: her intelligence

Flares, a post-coital cigarette
He doesn't share. That's it. He's watching her,
That's love for him: the eye. *Dinner yet?*
He shrugs. He's in no rush. She yawns. A blur
Of sunset colors. *Hold still. No, stretch.*
He's working now. He's busy on the sketch

She kicks one leg, pulls on a stocking, slow,
And then the other. She'll give him what he wants,
His private view. Later, in the studio,
Blotches on canvas. She can't praise what she can't
Admire. They'll quarrel. She'll say she was his muse.
Laughing, they'll strip. A burlesque. To amuse.

4. The Artist's Parents

Like a scene left out of *Traviata*:
Germond sits with his wife; their son observes
The proprieties, of dress, expression, cate-
Gorical refusal. *Better to serve
In hell*, he thinks, this prince, than reign here later.
Better to take a day job as a waiter.

That's thought, which always has its second act,
The wayward son brought back to heel by sheer
Sentiment and circumstance, the facts
Conspiring with morality and her
Acquiescence. She gives him up, gives in
So easily. A consciousness of sin,

We're meant to think. That's how a novel works;
Even a modern one. Step back a bit from pleasure;
What's left but manners, structure, laws, the quirks
Of capital, of which all art's the measure,
Not the undoing: mirrored above these faces,
The artist's love for just what he disgraces.

5. Writing the Letter

So tortured, she laughs, his language and the work
Of composition as she imagines it.
Why not speak plainly? Give the lead a jerk
To bring the pet to heel or stay or sit,
Then praise her or let her go. Not both or neither
At once. And be kind too. The smoother the leather

The better used, her father used to say,
Who knew his dogs and mares, and never once
Raised his voice or struck. He is a boy
To write me this, and, worse, he is a dunce
To think he should. We might have had a fine
Farewell, we two, regrets and bed and wine.

He must have written it pacing at his club.
Red drapes and mounted heads, the billiard balls
Clicking and the clock, his father's stubborn
Voice in one ear, his mother's sobs. When duty calls
He writes a really nasty piece of prose,
Dismissing her, and shrugs, and off he goes.

6. The Holy Well

She has a dream. She is a penitent,
Naked like the others she kneels on stone.
The well is healing. The well is sacrament,
Wholeness, wholly without self. *But lonely,*
Stripped (whose voice?); *unloved the self's unclad,*
Unclaimed. Who knew the tempter could sound so sad?

What of God's love? The book's a modern one.
Some answers don't occur, or seem *ad hoc.*
God, say. In the dream, she is alone
Despite the others there, souls on the rocks
Of loss or doubt or guilt or uncommitted
Sins, loves lost or made or unrequited.

The world being everything that is the case,
To lose any part of it... The beehive houses,
The bitingly blue sea, his face... His face,
On that wry man standing there, whom the scene rouses
To something like contempt, like the mockery
In her self-portrait as a dream's sincerity.

7. A Convent Garden, Brittany

Let's be clear; she's only visiting.
A holiday with a painter friend, who loves
The white of lilies, of novices, elicits
Nothing of her story, makes her move
To get a better light, makes her stare
Until the women and the flowers seem one prayer

Of simple being, doesn't give a damn
For gossip or much else, and over wine,
Baguettes, a local blue-veined cheese, smoked ham,
Says that beauty's anything that shines
In contrast with what most afflicts the heart.
Then laughs, picks up the bread, tears it apart.

She takes it, eats. She has a story to tell,
One she's not lived yet. That's how a novel goes:
Each act is predicated on a sequel.
A girl in white, her vows fresh as her clothes,
Moves toward the canvas's edge, and what she wants
Is where our eyes might go that her eyes can't.

Three Problems

1. The Problem with Remembering Baltimore in the Early Morning

— for John Drury

I do not believe that anything has changed.

Was it your apartment I stumbled to or mine
To play old records while our wives dozed?
They had jobs to get to, after all.

And we had the leisure to invent nostalgia. For what—
A few scratched 45s, a few hooks on organ and guitar before
the horns came in?
We were in the city where nothing is lost,

Not in the junk shops on the avenues, the jukeboxes of Fells
Point,
The 1950s hair and uniforms of the women behind the counter
of the diner,
The moon on the ceiling of the Famous Ballroom.
With so much present, why did we need to remember anything
at all?

I think The Four Tops are singing *Bernadette*
Or is it *Walk Away, Renee*?
I think the White Castle on Greenmount has finally closed, and
someone
Is misquoting Lacan again:
*The best image of the unconscious is Baltimore in the early
morning.*

The cab lights heading off down North Charles Street
Are the reflections of a bare bulb on the grooves of the lp

63

I found on the garbage trolley in the back stairway,

Ray Charles asking *Tell me what'd I say*
As if anyone could forget.

2. The Problem with the Poem About the Guitar

There are more strings than fingers, which makes scansion
difficult,
And the chords shift, diminished, augmented, as the words
bend the strings,
So subtle their weight, so acute the attention they require.

In a corner of the café, in a dark suit and battered felt hat,
In the occupied city, he plays *Honeysuckle Rose* with one
mangled hand
On the fretboard, one foot on his guitar case, nodding
To his *confrere's* rhythm, one eye on the door,
On the dark car idling at the curb.

Who will transcribe the chorus he plays before he slips out the
back way,
Through the kitchen, into the little hotel, past the concierge?
And the emptiness between the notes,
What hand will match the precision of his hand at rest?

As for the comping, *la pompe*, the turn-arounds and fills?
The rhythm of his guitar is beyond all measure, as history
shows,
And poetry, and any other record of our woes.

3. The Problem with Drinking Wine While Reading Chinese Poetry

— for Matthew Graham & after Tu Fu

When did we last sit on the riverbank and speak of the art of words?
Before this time of drought and flood, before the fall of the bureaucrats.
Who knew how much they were needed, how much we would miss
The smug consolations of exile,

So many odes to nothing, so many mayflies...
Now when I pick up the slender rod and cast among the evening shadows,
There is no peace, only this thin line of hunger.

As if, having learned of self-regard, it was time to consider justice.
As if a muffled bell sounded, not far enough off to ignore.

No Depression in Heaven

— dust bowl images in color at the Library of Congress

The revelation was the photographs
In color, like the famous ones, the epitaphs
For the common man, the dust bowl faces
We've gotten used to in black and white, all traces
Gone but shadow, as if the camera stole
The whole spectrum as well as soul's poor
Expectations. A bank can claim your deed,
A farm your hours, and a child your bread,
The photographer in his big Lincoln,
Like a bootlegger's, a kidnapper's,
The Speed Graphic cocked across his knees,
Can put you where you never meant to be.

B&W

I write in praise of the 35mm SLR,
The handy, ubiquitous Pentax K1000, or a Canon or Nikon,
The camera dangling from the hand of the guy in the striped t-
shirt and black jeans
On the cover of Dylan's *Highway 61*,

Slung over the shoulder of the woman in the Belstaff cycle
jacket
At the college art opening, the camera in *Blow-Up*
In David Hemmings' hands, around Catherine Leroy's neck in
Vietnam,
As the AP saw it and the UPI. As *Time* saw it, and the *Times*, and
Ramparts,

Frame by frame because someone twisted the lens into focus
At the motel, the ballroom, the park,
Unretouched, on the handbills, the walls of galleries and cafes,
You could buy film at any drugstore,

And step into the street, stand on the edge of things, the surge
As the police moved in, or the quiet doorway of a barn,
Just there, where the buckled plank wall divides light from dark,

All creation framed in degrees of shadow, and all god's witness.

Listening Room

— *for Charlie Haden, Rochester NY, 1970*

In the listening room
Of the Rundel Library
I let the needle fall
On *Change of the Century*.

Free jazz, a friend had said.
I wanted to be free,
Of what, I wasn't sure.
Outside, the Genesee

Rollicked down its flume,
Intransigent and lovely,
Below the National
Casket Company's

Sign, worn black on red.
Ramblin', Una Muy
Bonita, something pure,
An anonymity

And then the bass, strings pulled
Past pitch, past entropy.
And being here, just here,
Was gone, with them, with me.

Northern Lights

— Fairport, New York, 1972

Who saw them first, after our band practice, the green, silver-
edged dancers
Above Bill's mother's gravel driveway and her big Buick
The summer of our senior year,
Flaring up from the horizon, gaining height with indirection,
With patience?

Behind that scrim of charge and discharge
The stars I'd grown so used to, from songs, from graduation
exhortations,
Were dim,

But not gone, and so I took for a sign
What was meant for a lesson, as we all mistook promise
For those promises, the unspoken ones, the ones we meant to
keep,
And did, but by patience, by indirection,

And only remembered later. Here's one.
A friend I had not yet met was driving through upstate that
night
Heading for a teaching job and years of complicated trouble,
The sort you get into when intention isn't the half of it,
And he saw those lights too and put them in a poem

That I read aloud one day when I only thought I had forgotten
That between sign and accident is the slenderest of difference,
As between what we meant to do and what we did
Anyway.

Pour Me Another Cup of Coffee

—for it is the best in this land (Terry Fell, "Truck Drivin' Man")

Is the song on the Bluetooth speaker, but even as I write, it feels
like a false start, although the coffee is good this morning, and
I'm reading Paul Blackburn's *Journals*, so the trivial

Shouldn't be; he had such a graceful way with words and his son
and the trees at Cortland State and a friend's eighteenth
birthday hangover,

You forgot he knew how close death was, since love was closer,
took in so much. Maybe if I still smoked, or got up less to fire up
the coffee, I'd have the patience of a café writer, for whom the
world is a sufficient display,

Or if I hadn't lived so long between the burned over district and
a bookshelf buckling under the Transcendentalists, I'd be able to
forget about significance or its summoning or nostalgia

Which gives everything recalled that jukebox glow. But what I
really remember is how anyone could walk over, put in a
quarter and punch the buttons, and it was a take it or leave it
deal for the rest of the bar,

And how I never walked out, not even at the worst schlock,
because once in a while it would be Janis singing, as she did the
summer he died, *Get It While You Can*, coincidence, sure, but
good enough to be going on with

Until I figured out that I always got it a little too late, when what
no longer mattered was exactly what I was doing in memory, as
it turned out,

Of what I might have done: hitchhike downstate to Cortland,
say, and leave a bottle of something on the porch of a poet
who, too ill to drink, still knew gratitude when he saw it.

Café Central

*— What difference does it make what you talk about with a
poet; you're talking with a poet...* (Peter Altenberg)

I like the photo of myself
In the Café Central—*echt* American,
Plaid shirt, guidebook open,
A mélange and apricot pastry.
I like the waiter's affable precision;
He's *chi*, embodied,
Right action without consequence.

And the seated statue of Peter Altenberg,
At the front table, amused
That he outlasted Trotsky and even Freud
Who left after his feud with Adler,
And that when I pull out my phone
I slip and take a picture
Of my feet in black sneakers,

That I've never heard of him,
That sitting here I've missed a hundred details
That would have gone straight into his notebook,
Never to be revised
Since where's the pleasure in second thoughts?
Pleasure. He smiles, as who would not
On such a day, in such a spot.

A Little *Macbeth*

Goes a long way. On the Saturday broadcast
On the way home from the grocery store, the witches—
Not three voices, but three choruses, the announcer says,
And trained to screech, *swarm from the woods*
To preach lies (sort of) to power. And I might be tempted too,
To sit in the driveway, to listen to how it all comes to light,
Jung's collective unconscious, but so singular in how
We bear it, bear it forth. Until, of course, Verdi
Hams it up—he can't resist those pizzicatos, those
Piccolos, those you've-got-to-hum-it melodies—
And though the voice over's back, telling us how
In the third act all *apparitions*, mute or lyric
Will be revealed, here's this astounding early spring
Heat wave, a shimmer of new buds, and as welcome
As simple prophecy: the space between bare trees
Dwindles, and is it just the summer or are they moving
Towards us, into the emptiness some king has left,
And not to crown the oak or bristling pine,
But only because the same chorus I can't see anywhere
Has fallen silent to summon them.

Macbeth Revisited

— I had else been perfect...

The truth is, there was no one who did not know, not after
discovery of the gutted king.

The truth is, it was just the usual protocol of dynastic transfer,
centuries of it,

Assassination, massacre, one headman shrugged off by the
next, the next, one man's grave become another's dung heap,

And no one spared, and the sacrifice no longer to any goddess,
but only to ambition,

When Macbeth panics, it is always and only because that having
taken one step, he takes another.

All he had to do was sit in the shadows and listen to whatever
the women were singing around the fireside when they thought
themselves alone.

She had spent her time there, his lady,

And did not need the sisters to tell her what the ballads already
had, that murder is the king's business; who does it best is king
hereafter,

Until the next comes and washes his hands of him.

Ireland

1. The Thighbone of St. Feochan

— for Nat

I was in Taaffe's with my son, and the session was just beginning
To find its way past all that seriousness and the player's good
Intentions, the two self-conscious fluters and the poker-
Faced piper pushing the reels like water under a mill
Wheel, when the girl smiled, sat down, broke out
Her concertina, and they were away then, and so
Was I, cider forgotten on the bar behind me, and then
He punched my arm by way of hello, the old guy
In a cheap windbreaker and cotton cap, though outside
It was gusts and rain, and he had a lot to say on subjects
Large and small and most of it at some variance
With anything I'd think even once to say in a public house,
And he told me twice how good the music was that neither
Of us could hear a note of now that he was under steam
About his years in the merchant marine and the damned
Immigrants, and that, I told my son, when I grabbed him
By the arm and hauled us out of there, is just the way it goes,
You think you've heard the music of the spheres or
At least some minor variation that makes a favorite tune
Lift from the mists like the abbey of some saint whose name
You don't quite believe, and there's a relic, they say, holy
And approachable, but when you get there, the sign reads
The Thighbone of St. Feckin, another good bad joke
On the tourist you've become out of sheer hope.
And then some bastard wants to tell you how Capetown's gone
To hell for a sailor ever since, while the band is still
Trying to make themselves heard. You know the tune:
The Mills Are Grinding. You know you could play it
The rest of your life and still not make it right.

2. The Pleasing Prospect

— *in the exquisite clarity, every detail is visible*
(George Moore, on Ashford Castle)

Of the half-barbaric lough beyond the barbered lawn,
Is someone's hand at work, at welcome, and you might think
The author had this particular light of mind in mind: after
A morning's drizzle and attendant mists and a walk
From the abbey's gravestones, that the clouds would shift
Enough dull gravity to allow (this is a landscape that invites
Another century's allegory) hope to imbue the picturesque
With... Well, you can imagine for yourself the grandiosely
Detailed painting, an academician's folderol, failed but
Unfailingly polite, retired from salon to dusty country house
Wall, and left for our gently condescending pleasure
Before the server brings the bill. On the Shannon bus,
There was a drug deal going down in the back seat,
Three boys making sure we all knew to the penny
What ecstasy costs, and so much for all those postcard
Views, until we dropped them at the depot lot by a gas station.
And if I thought then how traveling seems to get you exactly
Nowhere, now let's raise a glass in this wood-paneled room
To wishful thinking, while all that sublime pity and terror
Slides into abeyance, such a good word for our tenancy
Of expectation in a world that is always someone else's estate,
And if by some accident or oversight or slight deceit
We got in that door, we might as well take the seat they offer
And all we never but the pleasing prospect could afford.

3. Talking about Taoist Precepts with Adrian Frazier

— Give up learning and put an end to your troubles

We can't. But since when is good advice that goes unheard
The *Tao* that *can* be told?--not the eternal walk along
The strand, each new footfall an act of balance
In the awkward, glinting, shifting stuff of it, the lark's
Warbling, meaningless and pleasing just by that,
None of that "irritable reaching after fact," and no
Ideas in the emptiness of things passed or past.
Be like a reed, the precepts say, and you're thinking
Of the trout at the current's margin, flecked and sipping
In the weeds (*be*), while I'm hearing some finicky,
Raucous instrument suddenly finding tune, the split
And doubled tongue (*a reed*) resolving, a sad
Philomelan voice and a drone suggesting that maybe
The point is *like*, resemblance teaching what learning can't
Acquire here among the rushes in a world of splendidly
Unnerving almost-rhymes (*rush* to *lush* to *loss* to *less* to
Summer's *lease*) we only have to half-remember
Since everywhere the reminders flock, call, and gyre.
Listen, we heard them once, the snippets, these
Brief bouts of wisdom, and though the studious might
Have set about transcribing them for posterity,
We watched the tide erase the plovers' tracks
And that was enough to send us home, uncork
At our ease a spirit whose sheer, lingering immediacy
Was smoke on the tongue for anyone who ever
Told us once we shouldn't have to be told twice.

Cornetists

— *for Marvin Bell*

They were the heroes once, in tunics of red or navy, gold trim
and buttons, epaulets and sharp-brimmed braided caps,

In the gazebos of village parks or on the stages of the vaudeville
and opera houses, those elegant little music boxes in the
industrial burghs,

Or in the city concert hall above the bank, packed with wool and
fur collars, the men's hats hanging upside down from the neat
racks under the wooden seats, and outside a biting early
November chill, a gust of snow.

Even then the cornet's voice was deep summer, the high
shimmer of light breaking on a conservatory's glass roof, the
valves and pistons of a steam launch heading to the great house
on the island, the flag rippling on the stern,

And the cadenza was the racing fleet tacking, the naval training
ship with the midshipman smart in their uniforms, the sublimity
of rhetoric that sends the crowd on its way, uplifted,
determined,

Flushed as they walked out to the street, the wind harsh off the
river, to the taproom or home for a hot whiskey or cider.

Already they missed it, the radiance of that sound, the cornet's
golden bell; they tried to conjure it up, but it was gone with the
evening, in the smell of strong spirits, the sound of a brawl
breaking out over what...

And now it is the mirror at the end of a long hallway of a house
in which they are no longer welcome, this nostalgia as they set
out,

Even with all those tasks before them, whistling a tune they have already half-forgotten.

John Brown's Dream

John Brown dreamed the devil was dead

He isn't. In North Elba with his freedmen, he sleeps poorly, the
old man.

Should God's war be a border feud, as if men were cattle, men
were reivers?

Who might tell them apart? Who would be safe from slaughter;
who numbered for it.

And judgment, as the whirlwind proclaimed, is an afterthought,
an impertinence, where dwells the devil

In doubt and impermanence, in human judgment, but he is
dead. And God is an armory to be plundered,

And freedom, above all else, a cleansing. He will make peace a
by-word.

A shard in the storm's coils. And that shall be equality, he
dreams, the end of difference,

Which is, God answers from his still point, the dream a man
who dies for it may have,

When he also dreams that the devil, who is only the work of our
hands, is dead.

The Fall

After the fall, I expanded my vocabulary: *syncope*, which
sounded languishingly Victorian, except for its "rapid onset and
quick recovery,"

And *positional vertigo*, explained by "shifting particles in the
inner ear." I thought it had a good, relativistic touch, quite
modern,

As if every point of view encoded its own doubt. And that's how
self-absorbed I was, from the ER to the MRI to the EKG,

And the operating assumption that nothing much seemed
wrong, even when the symptoms persisted

At odd times, the world like an old-fashioned film projector
stuttering between frames. I became a connoisseur of that
moment,

Finding analogues in Oliver Sacks and photo magazines and acid
memoirs. Not that they mattered, all these modes of defense,

If I were supposed to value life more after a close call, when all
each new day had to show me was how cheaply other lives
were held.

I was lying on the couch when the news came on with the
photos of the dead, and I rolled over to see better,

And though the world was spinning, those few frames just
ground to a halt.

The Moment of Contemplation

In the *Mahabharata*, when Arjuna and Krishna speak of action
and non-action on the eve of the battle, on the edge of the field
of Kurukshetra,

Do the watchers grow impatient, the horses stamp and snort,
the Kshatriyas whet their weapons?

Time is poised like a drawn bowstring. You cannot tell if that
tension quivers from the bow's desire or the archer's.

Time knows who will take the blame. Who else is there, so
imperishable, impersonal.

Time holds the next book of the epic like a vase above a tile
floor, the beautiful floor of a palace

Over which a war must be fought, a discord of cousins, of right
action conceived as duty, which is to say as disaster,

As widows and fires, a bed of arrows, a long discourse on
wisdom

That almost puts the listener to sleep, it is so soothing to think it
all might be sorted after such a great winnowing.

And then we have the chapters concerning illusion.

Another Problem with Mindfulness

The demons prefer the middle slopes, after the first hard
scramble as the elevation rises,

And you think you are used to the air of the high approaches.
Who can say which they desire more, your fatigue or that false
confidence (which is to say, your desire),

When, at the top of the escarpment, you look back to survey
the path so far and, pleased to see the bright nylon tents of
base camp so far below, forget to ponder

The barrenness of the next ascent, the slip of soles on scree, the
badly placed ladders on the cliffs that lead to the caves,

Which are themselves snares for the unwary, for who else
would come so far, poorly translated guidebooks in the rucksack
pocket, prayer flags tied hopefully, thoughtlessly to the cinch
straps.

When the old man at the junction where you jumped off the
train, the one with the goat's head fiddle, sang his one-string
song

About how wisdom is always the lesser path, why did you turn
away when that tattoo on his arm, the spiral mapping the Great
Descent,

Was all the warning you might need, and better than those
encounters told of in the commentaries, where the pilgrim, lost
in uncertainties, is pointed ever upwards by that most
untrustworthy of sages,

The one whose face ripples on the surface of that little spring where you bowed to drink so reverently before you tackled the first ascent.

With a Glass of Finger Lakes Red

Winifred Smith,1917-2011

Summer 1964,
Ten years old, drowsy, bored
In the catspaws on Canandaigua Lake,
I could hear the halyards shake,
See the telltales flutter, shift
As wind freshened off the shale cliffs
Of the Bristol Hills. The mainsail slacked
Then filled, the hull heeled as we tacked.
I held the jib. Dad, smoking, perched
On the foredeck, half on watch
To see I kept things trim. Mom
Had the tiller. It was her calm
Pleasure I remember best,
Repeating the words for me, the mast
And gunwales, the centerboard shackle,
The frayed wire stays, the boom's worn tackle,
Names for the boat, the lake, the weather.
In memory, love and naming tethered;
She's in the low sun, bow splash, rope
On the palm, waves' pitch and slope,
A few high cumuli barely looming.
Her arm rests on the cockpit coaming.
And sunset is a local wine
Like this one, sweet and full, entwined
With shale and silt, the long, thin lake,
A sailboat, a mother, and their wake.
Sleepy, the boy lets the jib sheet fall,
The canvas luff, feels the hull stall
Until she takes both sails in hand,
Course set, no hurry, back towards land.

The Dream of the Quarry

The night I knew my mother would be dying
I dreamed the dream again, but differently.
A small-town square, cobbled streets, close houses,
A labyrinth of lanes, and mews, and closes,
The kind of doorways you might see in Dublin,
But this was on a height above the Hudson.
This time I was no tourist, drawn to the windows
Of shops or down streets where the vista dwindled
Beyond the dream's permission. I wanted home,
Somewhere beyond the river's cliffs: homecoming.
The fog was thick. The road I took led upward,
Past rising shale, dead-ending in a quarry.
There was one door, a hall of seated children
Silent in rose red robes, in meditation.
(The night before I'd dreamed of a temple carved
Of rock that color, elaborate, barbaric,
A place of sacrifice, panic, assassins,
But this was worse, so calm, as if redemption
Meant letting go at last of all we'd loved,
Meant admitting the world was stone, unmoving.)
I left, more lost, climbed a wooden scaffold
Near the wall's top. On the river below, a gaff-rigged
Sloop was tacking upstream, upwind, and heeling.
Remember how for Christ the world unreeled
Below him as the tempter offered thrones,
Powers, dominions, the conclusion half-foregone,
Half balanced like a foot on a ladder's rung,
No place to put it right that wasn't wrong

Driving Up to Walton

Driving up to Walton, to see my mother's grave.
Driving up to Walton, going to see my father's grave.
Fog on the Cohocton. Main Street just repaved.

Detour past the drug store, flagmen and one lane closed.
Stuck in the detour past the drugstore, flagmen and one lane
closed.
Old music on the cd. I've got nothing but time to lose.

The plot's deed was in Dad's files, from 1922
Signed by his father, sometime in 1922.
They had that kind of foresight. I don't know that I want to.

I could take a walk down Main Street, buy a suit of clothes,
A hat with a crown ribbon, a cane, some fancy shoes.
 I could take a walk down Main Street, strike that ragtime pose,

Like the folks in the sepia picture taken at the depot here.
Bowlers, cravats, and frock coats, down at the depot here.
Dressed for some kind of frolic. The cloudy mirror

In my house was theirs, the railroad lantern, the clock.
All this stuff in my house, the railroad lantern, the clock.
The silhouette that might be mine, slouched, hands in pockets.

I don't even know the names, maybe just one or two.
I don't know how they died, except for one or two.
Rheumatic fever or train wrecks, war, the Spanish flu.

But here they are around me, Launts, Smiths, St. Johns.
They're here, around me. Jordans, Crosbys, St. Johns,
As at a formal party, introductions, stifled yawns,

A child pushed forward by elders, expected to recite.
A child pushed forward by his elders. They want him to recite
Something for the occasion, something to put things right.

It's Whitman. He's memorized it. He takes a breath,
As Whitman might, in memory, in fellowship, take a breath.
The smallest sprout shows there is really no death.

I put that on their headstone. I don't know if they'd approve.
I put that on their headstone. I don't know if they'd approve.
I don't know if I believe it, but I think that it's enough.

ACKNOWLEGEMENTS

Poems in this collection have appeared in:

Agni (The Fall: One Too Many Samurai Movies)

The Antioch Review (Soldier)

The Cincinnati Review (A Convent Garden, Brittany)

Cultural Weekly (Pour Me Another Cup of Coffee)

The Free State Review (B&W)

Live Encounters Writing & Poetry (Across the Street from the Miro Foundation; Early Music; Grandeur; Traverso; Northern Lights)

Like Light: Twenty-Five Years of Poetry and Prose by Bright Hill Writers (Yardman; Academe), Bright Hill 2017

Nine Mile (America, A Trance; Lorca's Mercedes)

Numero Cinq (On the Suicides at the NY/Canada Border; A Little *Macbeth;* Who Would Have Thought the Saxophone; With a Glass of Finger Lakes Red)

One (Little Black Train; The Thighbone of St. Feochan)

Salmagundi (*Pays du Haut;* Another Problem with Mindfulness; The Holy Well)

Smartish Pace (The Problem with Remembering Baltimore in the Early Morning)

Tupelo Review (Fuck)

Watching My Hands at Work: A Festschrift for Adrian Frazier (Talking about the Taoist Precepts with Adrian Frazier), Salmon 2013

Six of the poems in Eight Hats were included in *Hat & Key*, a limited edition of broadsides with poems by Jordan Smith and paintings by Walter Hatke, printed by Four Color, Inc., with support from Union College

**For a complete list of Three Mile Harbor Press books,
please visit us at: www.3mileharborpress.com**